The French Revolution

Terror and Triumph

Heather E. Schwartz

Publishing Credits

Dona Herweck Rice, *Editor-in-Chief*
Lee Aucoin, *Creative Director*
Torrey Maloof, *Editor*
Neri Garcia, *Senior Designer*
Stephanie Reid, *Photo Researcher*
Rachelle Cracchiolo, M.S.Ed., *Publisher*

Image Credits

cover Bridgeman Art Library; p.4 The Granger Collection; p.5 Getty Images; p.6 (left) Bridgeman Art Library, p.6 (right) Bridgeman Art Library; p.7 The Granger Collection; p.8 The Granger Collection; p.9 (top) Bridgeman Art Library, p.9 (bottom) Bridgeman Art Library; p.10 The Granger Collection; p.11 (top) The Granger Collection, p.11 (bottom) Bridgeman Art Library; p.12 Bridgeman Art Library; p.13 (top) The Granger Collection, p.13 (bottom) The Granger Collection; p.14 The Granger Collection; p.15 The Granger Collection; p.16 The Granger Collection; p.17 The Granger Collection; p.18 Bridgeman Art Library; p.19 Bridgeman Art Library; p.21 (top) Bridgeman Art Library, p.21 (bottom) Bridgeman Art Library; p.22 Alamy; p.23 Bridgeman Art Library; p.24 Bridgeman Art Library; p.25 The Granger Collection; p.26 The Granger Collection; p.26 iStock; p.27 Bridgeman Art Library; p.28 Bridgeman Art Library; p.29 (top) The Granger Collection, p.29 (bottom) Bridgeman Art Library; p.32 The Granger Collection; back cover Getty Images

Teacher Created Materials

5301 Oceanus Drive
Huntington Beach, CA 92649-1030
http://www.tcmpub.com
ISBN 978-1-4333-5011-5
© 2013 Teacher Created Materials, Inc.
Made in China
YiCai.032019.CA201901471

Table of Contents

peasant family

The Rising Tide of Revolution

Imagine that you are a French **peasant** living in the 1700s. You are poor, hungry, and angry. While you and your family suffer, the **nobility** are eating well and spending lots of money. You have to pay taxes to support the government, but the nobility does not.

This is what life was like before the French Revolution. In France, the king had all the power. There were no limits to what he could do. The people of France did not always like the king's decisions, but they could not vote. They had no say in who their rulers were or how their country was run.

The peasant class had no voice in its government, but strong leaders soon began to emerge. These people were willing to fight for change. They wanted a say in government and equality for all men. This fight became a violent struggle that lasted 10 years. It would not only change the government but French society as a whole. This struggle was called the French Revolution.

the American Revolution

Strict Social Classes

During the eighteenth century, French society was divided into three estates, or classes. The First Estate was the **clergy**, and the Second Estate was the nobility. These first two estates made up about three percent of the population. The remaining 97 percent of the population was poor peasants. They were known as the Third Estate.

Nobles and clergy had many **privileges**. They owned land but did not pay land taxes. They were also well educated. Peasants had no privileges. They paid taxes to the king and their lords. They also paid dues to the church. Peasants were not educated. Most could not read or write.

A peasant woman prepares a meal.

A noble family sits down to eat.

Peasants farm the land.

The Age of Enlightenment

The Age of Enlightenment was a period that led to the French Revolution. Writers and thinkers began to express new ideas about politics, religion, and science. Their ideas encouraged the French people to reconsider the country's social structure.

Struggling to Survive

The peasants had very tough lives. They had very little money because of all the taxes they had to pay. They had very little food to eat or sell. If their crops failed, they often starved. Life was so hard that many peasants did not live past 30 years of age.

Peasants were allowed to farm on land owned by the wealthy classes, but they did not have much control over their own work. They were forbidden to kill animals that ate their crops. The wealthy landowners wanted the animals alive so they could hunt them. Peasants could not stop landowners from hunting near or even on their crops. Landowners sometimes damaged peasants' crops or fences while hunting. If that happened, the landowners were not required to repair the damage or help the peasants in any way. Peasants had no power.

The Monarchy

A Young King

On May 10, 1774, King Louis XV (LOO-ee) died of smallpox. His son and oldest grandson had already died. Thus, the throne was passed to his younger grandson, Louis XVI. Louis XVI never wanted to rule France, but there was no escaping his fate. France now had a new, young king. Louis XVI and his wife, Marie Antoinette (an-twuh-NET), lived in the Palace of Versailles (ver-SAHY).

King Louis XV

Louis **inherited** a country in trouble. France was nearly **bankrupt** after losing the Seven Years' War. Its resources were strained. The population had grown from 20 million to 28 million during the eighteenth century. The people of France were poor and hungry.

When Louis XVI took the crown, he was only 19 years old. He did not have a strong, **decisive** personality. He was better known for being clumsy, awkward, and weak. Still, the people of France embraced him and Marie Antoinette as their new king and queen and hoped for changes that would improve their lives.

Instead, Louis made things worse by mismanaging the country's finances and making poor decisions. The peasants became angry. The streets of France filled with riots, lootings, and lynchings.

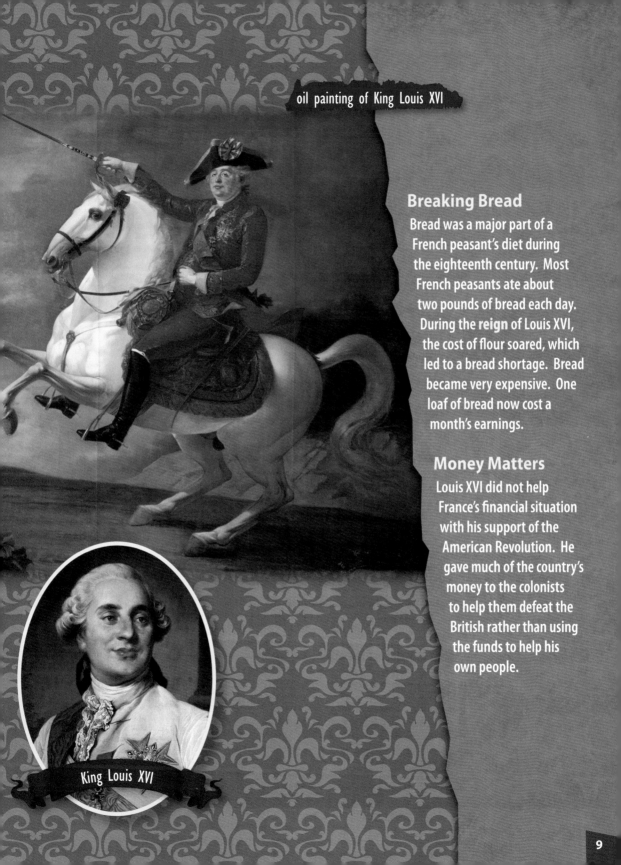

oil painting of King Louis XVI

Breaking Bread

Bread was a major part of a French peasant's diet during the eighteenth century. Most French peasants ate about two pounds of bread each day. During the **reign** of Louis XVI, the cost of flour soared, which led to a bread shortage. Bread became very expensive. One loaf of bread now cost a month's earnings.

Money Matters

Louis XVI did not help France's financial situation with his support of the American Revolution. He gave much of the country's money to the colonists to help them defeat the British rather than using the funds to help his own people.

King Louis XVI

Madame Deficit

Soon the people of France were not happy with their new king and queen. They were starving and suffering while the young queen, Marie Antoinette, was buying all the latest fashions and wearing fancy hairstyles. She spent her time dancing and attending the opera. She **gambled** with the country's money. The people of France felt that she was not helping them or their country. Marie Antoinette's **extravagant** lifestyle earned her the nickname "Madame Deficit."

Marie Antoinette

The French people found another reason to dislike Marie Antoinette. For the first eight years of her marriage, she did not have any children. As queen, it was her duty to produce an heir. This heir would take the throne after King Louis XVI. Later, between 1778 and 1786, Marie Antoinette did have two sons and two daughters. As her family grew, she became a less extravagant queen. She devoted more of her time to her children.

However, the people of France had already turned against Marie Antoinette. Their lives had not improved. They had lost confidence in the monarchy. It was too late for the queen of France to win back the affections of her people.

Petit Trianon

Petit Trianon

After she had her children, Marie Antoinette lived at Petit Trianon (PET-ee tree-AH-no). This was a retreat built on the grounds of Versailles. She enjoyed the privacy there, but the people of France were **suspicious** of a queen who needed privacy.

Media Mayhem

By 1783, illegal **pamphlets** about Marie Antoinette began to circulate and spread rumors. They claimed that the queen was behaving **immorally**. These pamphlets further damaged the queen's reputation. Although the pamphlets were illegal, there were so many that were printed that the government could not stop them.

Marie Antoinette and her children

The Revolution Begins

A Radical Move

By 1789, King Louis XVI knew he had to address France's problems. He called a meeting of the Estates-General. This political body had not met in 175 years. It represented France according to social class. The First Estate represented the clergy. The Second Estate represented the nobility. The Third Estate represented the peasants. Each estate was allowed one vote on issues.

The Estates-General met for several months to discuss the problems in France. The Third Estate felt unfairly represented. It represented most of the French population. Yet they were allowed only one vote. On June 17, 1789, the Third Estate made a **radical** move. They **defected**, or broke free, from the Estates-General. The Third Estate now called itself the National Assembly.

Estates-General at Versailles

the Tennis Court Oath

The Tennis Court Oath

King Louis XVI tried to stop the Third Estate from meeting as the National Assembly. The king locked them out of their meeting space. Instead of quitting, they moved to an old tennis court. At the meeting, they took an oath that they would write a new constitution for France. This oath was called the Tennis Court Oath.

A Leader for Democracy

Maximilien Robespierre (maks-uh-mill-IYAN ROHBZ-pee-air) was a leader of the Third Estate. He gained more power when he was elected to the National Assembly. He was prepared to fight for a more democratic government in France.

The National Assembly wanted the nobles and clergy to join them. The king quickly realized he could not control this new organization. On June 27, he gave in. He ordered the nobles and clergy to join the National Assembly. The people of France had won! And, this victory was only the beginning. In July, the National Assembly began writing a new constitution for their country.

Maximilien Robespierre

Storming the Bastille

King Louis XVI was willing to recognize the National Assembly. However, that did not mean he wanted to lose power to this new group. Encouraged by Marie Antoinette, he sent royal troops to keep the people of France under control. This decision made the people uneasy. They worried they were about to be attacked.

Next, Louis made another unpopular decision. He dismissed the country's well-liked director general of finances, Jacques Necker (zhahk NEK-er). Now, the people were angry. They wanted to fight back.

storming the Bastille

Jacques Necker

Necker Returns

Two days after the storming of the Bastille, the National Assembly demanded Jacques Necker be returned to his former position. King Louis XVI listened to the National Assembly and renamed Necker the Director General of Finances.

Dressing the Part

On July 17, 1789, Louis made a dangerous trip from Versailles to Paris. He knew the people of France were against him now. But he trusted them enough to believe they would not harm him. He showed goodwill by wearing the revolutionary colors: red, white, and blue.

On July 14, 1789, about 20,000 people stormed the Bastille (ba-STEEL). The Bastille was an ancient prison on the east side of Paris. To the people of France, it was a symbol of the monarchy's abuse of power. The people also knew they could find weapons there.

At the Bastille, the mob demanded weapons. The guards refused, and chaos broke out. The mob tore apart the building brick by brick and killed guards and the Bastille's governor, the Marquis de Launay (MAHR-key day LOW-nay). Afterward, they cut off his head, stuck it on a spike, and paraded it through the streets. It was a violent start to the French Revolution.

The Great Fear

All over France, peasants were hungry and angry. The storming of the Bastille inspired more riots in other towns during the summer of 1789. Many of the riots were violent. Mobs forced city officials out of their positions, and new town governments were formed. Regular citizens created their own military forces.

Rumors fueled the people's anger and fear. King Louis XVI appeared to be accepting of the revolution, but everyone expected him to fight back. Some said the king was plotting to have their crops burned and their villages destroyed. Others said the queen wanted to starve them. People began to falsely report sightings of the king's men around their towns. When this happened, a whole town could be thrown into complete chaos.

Peasants riot during the Great Fear.

Many peasants responded to these rumors with action. They burned landowners' homes and feudal (FYOOD-l) records that symbolized the taxes they had paid. Sometimes, they looted and murdered. France was out of control.

This period was later known as the Great Fear. The people had a lot to fear, as their streets had turned violent and chaotic and their king could not be trusted.

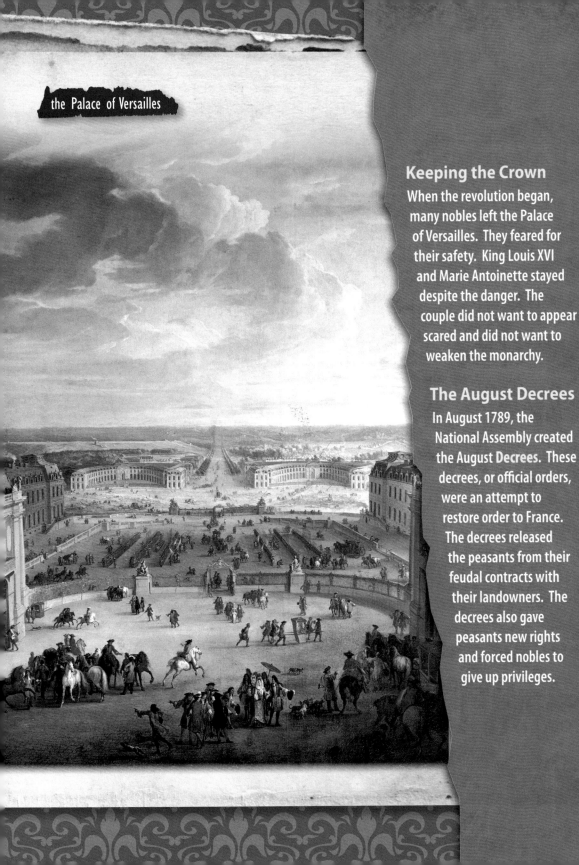

the Palace of Versailles

Keeping the Crown

When the revolution began, many nobles left the Palace of Versailles. They feared for their safety. King Louis XVI and Marie Antoinette stayed despite the danger. The couple did not want to appear scared and did not want to weaken the monarchy.

The August Decrees

In August 1789, the National Assembly created the August Decrees. These decrees, or official orders, were an attempt to restore order to France. The decrees released the peasants from their feudal contracts with their landowners. The decrees also gave peasants new rights and forced nobles to give up privileges.

A New Form of Government

A New Charter

On August 26, 1789, the National Assembly adopted a new charter for France. This list of articles was called the Declaration of the Rights of Man and the Citizen. It symbolized a radical change for France.

The country's old system of social classes was based on the idea of inequality. Peasants were not allowed the same rights and privileges as the clergy and nobility. The Declaration called all men of France free and equal. It said the government should work for the benefit of its people.

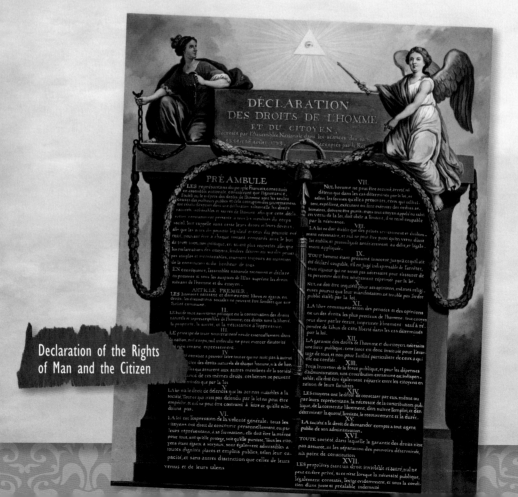

Declaration of the Rights of Man and the Citizen

The mob marches to Paris.

Defensive Move

The mob that marched to Versailles believed the king was planning an attack against them. Louis XVI was setting up new military troops at Versailles. They thought he would use them to attack Paris. In a defensive move, the mob decided to attack first.

Murderous Intent

When the mob stormed Versailles, the people intended to kill Marie Antoinette. They killed the queen's guards and placed their heads on spikes. The mob tore apart Marie Antoinette's bedroom but could not find her. Later, Marie Antoinette appeared on a balcony. She calmed the mob with her dignified manner.

The Declaration was a major step toward democracy in France. However, it put Louis XVI and Marie Antoinette in a dangerous spot. There was no place for royalty in a democracy.

In October, an angry mob gathered in Paris. Change was not coming quickly enough for the people of France, and they blamed the king and queen. The mob began to march to Versailles. The people carried brooms, pitchforks, and knives to use as weapons.

The mob forced the royal family out of the palace and brought them back to Paris where they could be watched. The family had become prisoners of the people.

The Legislative Assembly

In Paris, the royal family lived at Tuileries (TWEE-luh-reez) Palace. They had well-furnished rooms and servants. They still behaved and lived like royalty, but they were watched and guarded closely. Everyone knew King Louis XVI was against the revolution. He wanted to uphold the monarchy.

By September 1791, Louis had no choice but to swear his loyalty to the Declaration of the Rights of Man and the Citizen. Although his power was restored, he knew things would never be the same. The monarchy was lost.

Later that month, the National Assembly met to make it official. The country became a constitutional, or limited, monarchy. The king, who had always ruled alone, would now share his power with a newly elected **Legislative** Assembly. This assembly would replace the National Assembly.

On August 27, 1791, Austria and Prussia threatened France with military action. The two countries wanted to end the French Revolution. This threat was called the Declaration of Pillnitz (PEEL-neets). It asked European rulers to help the king of France. They wanted Louis restored to power. This threat would result in a war.

Tuileries

Traitor!

While at Tuileries Palace, the royal family felt their lives were in danger. In June 1791, they tried to escape to Austria. They were caught near the border and arrested. The family was brought back to Paris. The escape attempt made people think of King Louis XVI as a traitor. He had tried to abandon his country and his people.

The Case for War

The French people pushed for war against Austria. They felt war would destroy all those opposed to the revolution. Then, the changes they wanted would come more quickly.

In the background, the royal family attempts to escape.

The Revolution Ends

France at War

In September 1792, the National Convention was formed. It replaced France's Legislative Assembly. Its members were elected by vote. The National Convention wanted to **abolish**, or get rid of, the monarchy and put into effect a new constitution for France.

King Louis XVI had hoped Austria might help rescue his monarchy. But, the Legislative Assembly wanted to declare war on Austria. The country had threatened France. Austria insisted that France not harm Louis and give him back his power. Louis was no longer truly in charge of France. On April 20, 1792, he had to sign a decree declaring war on Austria.

The National Convention questions King Louis XVI.

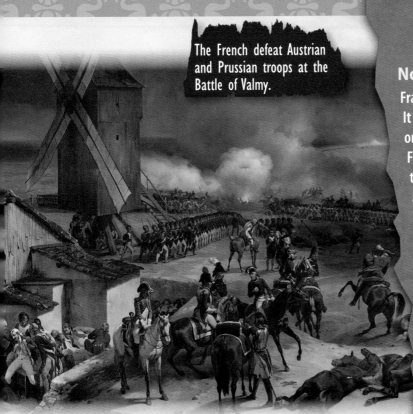

The French defeat Austrian and Prussian troops at the Battle of Valmy.

Not Ready for War

France was not prepared for war. It did not have enough supplies or officers to lead the soldiers. Furthermore, French soldiers sent to Austria had a revolutionary attitude. They questioned authority. When orders were issued, they voted on whether to follow them. They attacked and killed officers who tried to enforce the orders.

Girondins vs. Jacobins

The Girondins (juh-RON-deenz) were moderates who controlled the National Convention in the early months. Later, the Jacobins (JAK-uh-binz) took over. They were more radical and wanted more democracy. Their leader was Maximilien Robespierre.

The war was not going well for France. On July 25, 1792, the commander of the Austrian and Prussian armies issued a warning to the struggling country. This warning was called the *Brunswick Manifesto*. It said that France should restore the monarchy and that no harm should come to the royal family. If France did not obey, Austria and Prussia would attack and destroy Paris.

Despite the threat, the very next day, Maximilien Robespierre called for Louis's removal from the throne.

Death to the Monarchy

Not long after Robespierre called for the removal of King Louis XVI from the throne, the royal family was taken to the Temple Prison. Life at the prison was like nothing they had ever known. The rooms were cramped, airless, and dirty. Still, they were allowed large meals and money for clothing and furniture.

Marie Antoinette hoped the Austrian and Prussian armies would defeat Paris and rescue the monarchy. But, that was not to be. On September 22, 1792, the National Convention declared France was no longer a monarchy. It was now a republic. On December 11, 1792, Louis was put on trial for **treason**. In January, France's king was found guilty.

the royal family in the Temple Prison

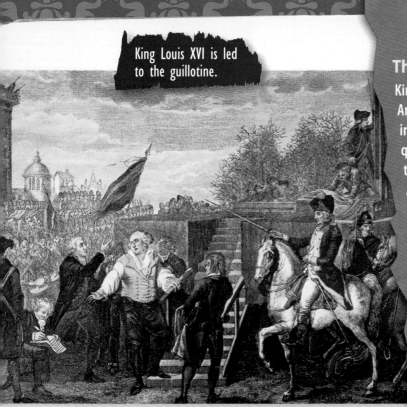

King Louis XVI is led to the guillotine.

King Louis XVI and Marie Antoinette's oldest son had died in 1789. When the king and queen were imprisoned, so were their two remaining children. After their parent's executions, the children remained in prison. Louis Charles died in prison in 1795 at the young age of 10. His older sister was sent to Austria when she was 17 in exchange for French prisoners.

The September Massacres

As the Austrian and Prussian soldiers approached Paris in early September 1792, the people of France became violent. They believed prisoners might get a chance to aid the enemy. To prevent this, they broke into prisons and murdered about 1,500 prisoners. This violence was called the September Massacres.

Louis was **executed** by a new device called a *guillotine* (GEE-uh-teen). The guillotine was designed to kill criminals swiftly and efficiently. It used a heavy blade that dropped down fast to slice off its victim's head. It was used in public so everyone could witness the punishment of criminals.

In October 1793, Marie Antoinette was also charged with treason. The court had no evidence against her, but she was found guilty. A large crowd gathered for her execution. As Marie Antoinette's head fell to the ground, the crowd cheered. The monarchy in France was dead.

Prisoners being held during the Reign of Terror

Reign of Terror

Maximilien Robespierre had now gained control over France. He ruled by **terrorizing** those who were against the revolution. France became a frightening place. Spies were everywhere. Anyone could be considered an enemy.

Minor **infractions** were considered suspicious. Some people were turned in for using the formal phrases *Monsieur* (muhs-YUR) or *Madame* (muh-DAM). In the new republic, they were supposed to call each other "Citizen." They also had to watch how they spoke about the revolution. They might be turned in if they did not sound passionate and supportive enough.

In June 1794, the Law of the 22nd Prairial (PREH-ree-ahl) was passed. It sped up the legal system. Enemies of the revolution now moved through the courts more quickly. That meant more executions. Between September 1793 and July 1794, over 17,000 people were put to death by guillotine. This period became known as the Reign of Terror.

Toward the end of Robespierre's reign, moderates began to take control of the country. Robespierre himself was executed on July 28, 1794. France entered a new period called the Thermidorian (thur-mi-DAWR-ee-uhn) Reaction.

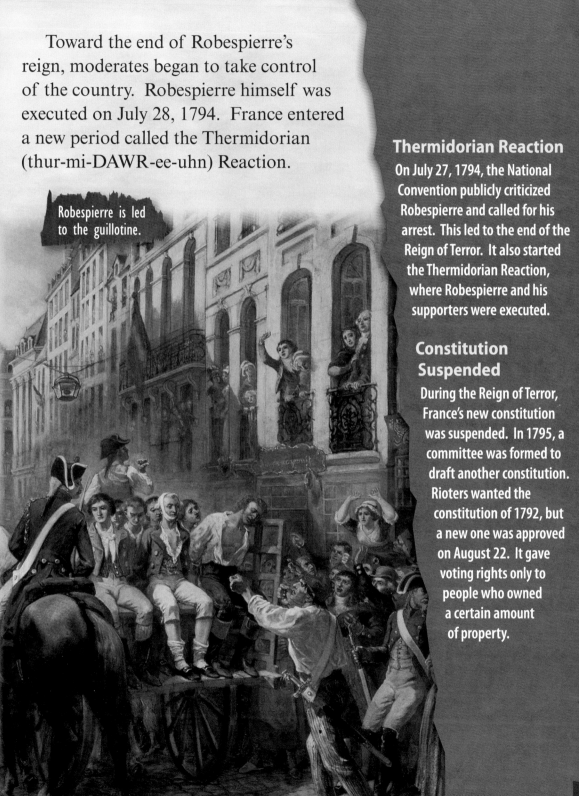

Robespierre is led to the guillotine.

Thermidorian Reaction

On July 27, 1794, the National Convention publicly criticized Robespierre and called for his arrest. This led to the end of the Reign of Terror. It also started the Thermidorian Reaction, where Robespierre and his supporters were executed.

Constitution Suspended

During the Reign of Terror, France's new constitution was suspended. In 1795, a committee was formed to draft another constitution. Rioters wanted the constitution of 1792, but a new one was approved on August 22. It gave voting rights only to people who owned a certain amount of property.

Napoleon's Rule

On October 26, 1795, military leader Napoleon Bonaparte (nuh-POH-lee-uhn BOH-nuh-pahrt) was named commander-in-chief of all armies in France. Military successes made Napoleon a hero in France. He defended France against enemies of the revolution. He helped to restore order in the country. However, he used his status to his own advantage. He was part of a military **coup d'etat** (koo dey-TAH). A coup d'etat is a plan to overthrow the government. The plan worked! Napoleon became France's new leader in November, 1799.

King Louis XVIII

The next month the French Revolution was officially over. Napoleon was named First **Consul** (KON-suhl). He **reformed** the country's educational, financial, and legal systems. He helped make France a leader in Europe. But Napoleon was also a **dictator**. He ruled with total power. He did not allow anyone to challenge his decisions.

Napoleon wanted to conquer the entire world for France. However, in 1814, Napoleon was removed from power after several military defeats. King Louis XVI's younger brother, Louis XVIII, came to France to claim the throne. After years of revolution, France's monarchy was restored in 1815.

Napoleon is defeated at the Battle of Waterloo.

Napoleon I

Another King

In 1802, Napoleon was made First Consul for life. This gave him absolute power, much like a king. But that was not enough for Napoleon. In 1804, he named himself Napoleon I, Emperor of France. The new title meant his power could be passed down through his family.

France's Democracy

After Napoleon's rule, it took more than a century for France to become a stable democracy where the people would have a say in their government.

Glossary

abolish—destroy; get rid of

bankrupt—lacking money to pay debts

clergy—the group of religious officials such as priests, ministers, or rabbis

constitution—the basic beliefs and laws of a nation

consul—a government official

coup d'etat—a sudden overthrowing of a government by a small group

decisive—having the ability to make decisions

decrees—orders signed by a ruler

defected—stopped supporting a cause or group

dictator—a ruler who has complete control, often cruel

dynasty—the lines of rulers that follow from families

executed—legally put someone to death

extravagant—beyond what is reasonable

gambled—played a game for money or property

guillotine—a machine for cutting off a person's head

immorally—not moral; wicked

infractions—disobedient acts

inherited—received something from someone who has died

legislative—a group that makes laws

moderates—a political group that has less extreme views

monarchy—a system of rule with a king or queen in power

nobility—people belonging to the upper class

pamphlets—short, printed, and unbound publications with no covers or with paper covers

peasant—member of the agricultural class

privileges—rights given to only certain people or groups

radical—extreme

reformed—made better

reign—a period of time when a ruler is in power

suspicious—not trusting

terrorizing—making people feel afraid

traitor—someone who is disloyal

treason—an act of disloyalty to one's country

Index

Your Turn!

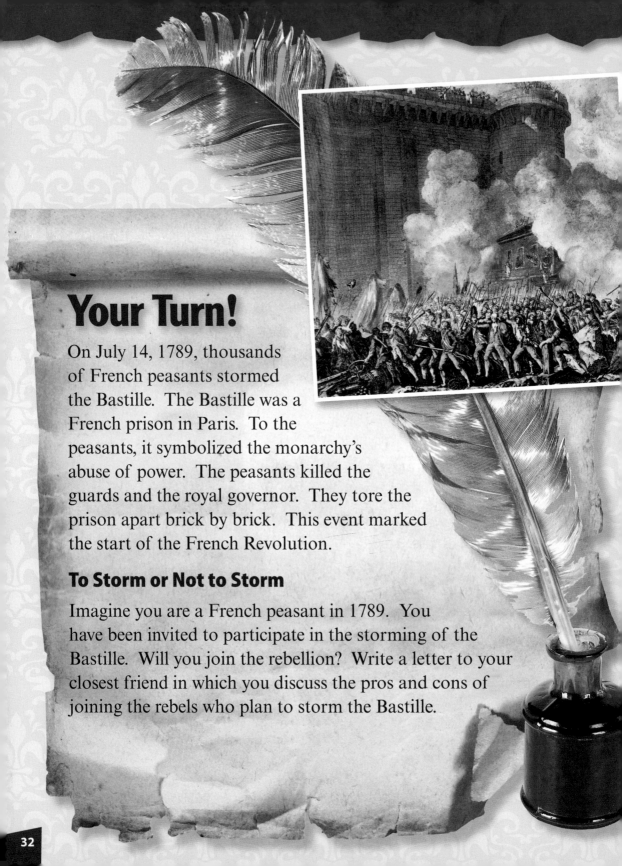

On July 14, 1789, thousands of French peasants stormed the Bastille. The Bastille was a French prison in Paris. To the peasants, it symbolized the monarchy's abuse of power. The peasants killed the guards and the royal governor. They tore the prison apart brick by brick. This event marked the start of the French Revolution.

To Storm or Not to Storm

Imagine you are a French peasant in 1789. You have been invited to participate in the storming of the Bastille. Will you join the rebellion? Write a letter to your closest friend in which you discuss the pros and cons of joining the rebels who plan to storm the Bastille.